ENDANGERED PLANTS

ALSO BY ELAINE LANDAU

ENDANGERED PLANTS

By Elaine Landau

A FIRST BOOK

NEW YORK   LONDON   TORONTO   SYDNEY

Cover photograph copyright ©: Mark W. Skinner/California Native Plant Society
Photographs copyright ©: Brent Wauer: p. 8; California Native Plant Society: pp. 12
(Robert Thorne), 22 inset, 36 (both Mark W. Skinner), 28 (Glen Clifton),
34 (Rick York); Mary Poulson: pp.: 16 top, 18, 19, 20; Bruce Palmer/ Arizona
Game and Fish Dept.: p. 16 bottom; Jo-Ann Ordano Photography: p. 22;
John Palis: pp. 24, 51; San Antonio Botanical Gardens: pp. 29 (Patty Leslie),
42 (Paul Cox); Mike Creel/South Carolina Wildlife and Marine Resources Dept.,
Columbia, S.C.: pp. 30, 32, 50; University of Hawaii at Manoa: pp. 38
(Dr. Gerald D. Carr), 40 (Dr. George K. Linney); Steven Q. Croy: p. 2, 44;
Bok Tower Gardens/Jonathan Shaw: p. 46.

Library of Congress Cataloging-in-Publication Data

Landau, Elaine.
Endangered plants / Elaine Landau.
p.   cm. — (A First book)
Includes bibliographical references (p.   ) and index.
Summary: Describes plants, such as the Catalina mahogany, dwarf
ilianus, and Okeechobee gourd, that are at risk of becoming extinct
and efforts to save them.
ISBN 0-531-20134-1
1. Endangered plants—United States—Juvenile literature.
2. Plant conservation—United States—Juvenile literature.
[1.Rare plants. 2. Plant conservation.] I. Title. II. Series.
QK86.U6L36   1992
581.5'29—dc20   91-34926 CIP AC

CONTENTS

ENDANGERED PLANTS

INTRODUCTION

Roses are red
Violets are blue
Or are they?

Despite their name, not all violets are bluish purple. Some *species* (types) of these flowers are also pink, white, or yellow. Yet recently, Brent Wauer, a Texas park ranger, came across a cluster of unusual yellow violets he'd never seen before. These blossoms hung from a steep limestone cliff in a wilderness park in Texas' Guadalupe Mountains. The ranger knew of no yellow-flowered plants in the area, so he felt certain that the violets were special.

As it turned out, the ranger had stumbled upon an extremely rare blossom known as the Guadalupe violet (*Viola guadalupensis*, scientific name). This flower is a survivor of the region's ancient rain forests. *Botanists* believe that most of these violets disappeared more than 8,000 years ago. The Guadalupe violet is now an *endangered* species. It represents the plight of many plants that are at risk of dying out or becoming extinct.

In the United States, nearly 3,000 plants are endangered. Most of these species are found in Arizona, Cali-

Guadalupe violet

fornia, Florida, Hawaii, Oregon, and Texas. A study by the Center for Plant Conservation warns that 680 endangered plants in the United States may no longer exist by the year 2000. In addition, tens of thousands of other plants are at risk throughout the world. Many endangered species in the tropics are already nearly extinct.

Often these plants have become endangered because of human activities. Apartment complexes, schools, shopping malls, and highways have all replaced vast tracts of fields and forests. Forests have also been destroyed to meet the lumber industry's need for wood. Plants prized for their beauty or unusual qualities are overpicked by collectors. At times, florists and plant suppliers also overcollect flowers and plant bulbs to ship to customers in many parts of the world.

Some plants are at risk due to overgrazing by both livestock and wild animals. Introducing new forms of vegetation has also often crowded plants out of their natural environments. Climate changes occurring over the years have taken their toll on some plants as well.

To try to save endangered plants in the United States, the government adopted the Endangered Species Act in 1973. The law prohibits importing or exporting endangered plants and bans the sale of these plants between the states. It also forbids collecting endangered plants growing on federal land or purposefully destroying these plants. In addition to the federal law, many states passed their own laws to protect endangered species within their borders.

Unfortunately, these measures have not been as effective as was hoped. A combination of poor funding and understaffing makes enforcing these laws difficult. There also seems to be a lack of public concern over preserving plants. Although plants have benefited people through the ages and are essential to keeping nature's balance, they may lack the appeal of many endangered animals. It is generally easier to raise support for a cuddly panda or a clever chimp than for a threatened tree or wildflower.

Nevertheless, we cannot afford to ignore their plight. Plant life is crucial to the earth's future. As the park ranger who found the nearly extinct yellow violet said, "To me this plant reflects a purity of nature that we desperately need. . . . We seem to be at war with our planet. If we win that war, we'll lose."

CATALINA MAHOGANY
(Cercocarpus traskiae)

The Catalina mahogany is among the rarest trees in North America. Today only seven grow in the rocky soil of Santa Catalina Island off Huntington Beach, California.

The tree's decline can be traced to the island's history. Nearly 4,000 years ago, when the area was inhabited only by Indians, Catalina mahogany trees were abundant. Then in 1542, the first European explorers arrived. Following the explorers, the island served as a haven for English pirates, Yankee smugglers, and Russian fur traders.

During the nineteenth century, groups of white settlers arrived on Santa Catalina. Some came seeking wealth, since gold was discovered on the island just before the California Gold Rush. Other settlers came to raise sheep, cattle, horses, and goats. To be sure there was room for the newcomers, the island Indians, Native Americans who had always lived in harmony with nature, were shipped to the mainland by government order.

Interestingly, the arrival of goats on the island is

Catalina mahogany

largely responsible for the near disappearance of the Catalina mahogany tree. The animals' overgrazing destroyed much of the island's natural vegetation. Once the plant growth protecting the soil was gone, the ground became less fertile.

The goats were aided in their destruction of island plant life by the settlers' large herds of sheep grazing on the same territory. To make matters worse, before long the numbers of wild pigs brought to the island by settlers began to multiply. These animals rooted out the local vegetation. Even the settlers played a role in destroying the island's trees and flowers. They chopped down trees for firewood and overpicked some of the most beautiful blossoms.

It is likely that the Catalina mahogany would be extinct, if it weren't for efforts made in the 1950s to reduce animal grazing and rooting on the island. Unfortunately, the program wasn't completely successful. A good deal of grazing continued, and once the bison and mule deer were brought to the island, the few remaining Catalina mahogany trees were seriously threatened.

To save the Catalina mahogany, in 1985 botanists built fencing around two of the mature trees. They were careful to leave a fair amount of space within the enclosed area for new growth. The project's results were extremely promising. By 1987, nearly seventy seedlings had begun to grow.

Cuttings were also taken from the adult Catalina mahogany trees. After the cuttings took root in a protected environment, the young seedlings were replanted in three open island areas. Although these young trees survived, some were partially eaten by deer. Efforts to protect the Catalina mahogany continue. Perhaps one day it will no longer be California's rarest tree.

PEEBLES NAVAJO CACTUS
(Pediocactus peeblesianus)

SILER'S PINCUSHION CACTUS
(Pediocactus sileri)

BRADY PINCUSHION CACTUS
(Pediocactus bradyi)

KNOWLTON'S CACTUS
(Pediocactus knowltoni)

In the high desert regions of New Mexico and Arizona grow cacti smaller than silver dollars. These petite plants bear colorful funnel-shaped flowers and have grayish spines that blend with their coarse rocky surroundings. Once these plants were plentiful, but today the tiny flowering cacti face *extinction*.

The cacti have grown scarce for several reasons. One is the extensive quarrying and mining done in the plants'

Peebles Navajo cactus

Brady pincushion cactus

Siler's pincushion cactus

natural environment. Other factors include cattle grazing and the off-road use of jeeps, trucks, and tractors.

Yet perhaps the greatest threat to the cacti is over-collecting by humans. As these small desert plants are in demand at floral shops, uprooting them for profit is a thriving business. Because the tiny cacti are extremely difficult to cultivate or grow outside their natural *habitats*, collecting efforts have been unusually broad.

To help these plants survive, botanists are studying the conditions necessary for their growth. This is crucial in working with heavily collected plants, so they can one day be grown in *greenhouses*, both to sell and to possibly be replanted in the wild. The botanists discovered that the cacti only grow in very dry, shallow, gravelly soil. They also thrive in climates with cold winters, cool wet springs, and very dry summers. In the desert, the cacti are aided by a soil *fungus*. The fungus clings to the plants' roots, helping them to better absorb both water and soil nutrients.

Armed with this information, botanists want to re-create the natural environment of the cacti in a controlled setting. Their work may help these tiny plants remain a part of the desert landscape.

Knowlton's cactus

RAVEN'S MANZANITA
(Arctostaphylos hookeri)

Raven's manzanita is an attractive, low-growing California shrub. The plant has shiny leaves and bears brownish berries. It is in grave danger of becoming extinct as only one shrub is left in the wild.

The single remaining plant is located on a U.S. Army base in San Francisco, California. These plants were once common in the area, but increased housing and business construction crowded them out.

Now the last shrub may be overrun by other vegetation growing at the same site. Raven's manzanita will only survive if the surrounding plants are properly weeded out and new sites for the threatened plant are begun with cuttings from the remaining plant.

Raven's manzanita

FLORIDA TORREYA
(Torreya taxifolia)

Over two hundred years ago, when the first European settlers arrived at the Apalachicola River Basin connecting Florida and Georgia, they saw seemingly endless acres of lush green forests. The trees stood up to 60 feet (18.3 m) tall and had leaves that looked like bright green needles. Blanketing the area's cool, steep slopes, these stately cone-bearing (*conifers*) trees were later named Florida torreyas.

At one time, the trees may have occupied a large portion of eastern North America. But during the last ice age, they were pushed south. When it was over, Florida torreyas grew only in the Florida-Georgia river basin.

The Florida torreya was valued both for its beauty and its usefulness. Its wood retained its strength and attractiveness through the worst weather. Ideally suited for outdoor use, the lumber was frequently fashioned into fence posts and house shingles.

These majestic trees thrived until the 1950s. Then botanists noticed that disease-producing fungi were attacking them. The forests disappeared as the lethal fungi killed large numbers of the trees. The few that remain are

Florida torreya

mostly new trees sprouting from the roots of the dying growth. But the fungi soon strike the young trees, killing them as well.

Botanists are studying fungal diseases to try to stop the destruction. So far they have learned that at least six types of fungi have hurt the trees. They also discovered that smoke acts to inhibit fungus growing in the wild, and they are designing a smoke screen to halt the diseases' spread. The use of poisons to kill the fungi is also being considered.

Besides efforts to save the Florida torreya in its natural environment, botanists hope to grow new trees from existing tree cuttings. These young plantings will be *cultivated* in controlled environments and later planted in suitable botanical gardens.

The story of the Florida torreya raises important questions about what may be necessary to save some endangered species. Preserving a plant's natural environment is not always enough. Although many Florida torreyas grew on government land, their safe haven couldn't protect them from disease. Further research, disease control, and new growth projects are vital to this regal tree's survival.

SERPENTINE SUNFLOWER
(Helianthus exilis)

PUZZLE SUNFLOWER
(Helianthus paradoxus)

SCHWEINITZ'S SUNFLOWER
(Helianthus schweinitzu)

Sunflowers beautify the landscape throughout much of the country. Varieties of these flowers may be spotted near the New Jersey shore, in remote New Mexico deserts, on California sand dunes, in western Texas marshes, and in other areas. Sunflowers have a large disk center surrounded by a fringe of yellow petals. Although some sunflowers are more than a foot (.3 m) wide, other types are quite small.

Sunflowers are an important part of America's floral heritage. Over two hundred years ago, Native Americans made an oil from the flower heads. Early Spanish settlers used sunflowers to make meal or gruel. They also obtained black and purple dye from sunflower seeds and yellow dye from its petals.

Above: Serpentine sunflower
Facing page: Puzzle sunflower

Today, several types of sunflowers have become extremely scarce. Among these are the serpentine sunflower, puzzle sunflower, and Schweinitz's sunflower.

The serpentine sunflower exists only in a few sites in northern California. What remains of its environment is further threatened by regional gold mining. The serpentine sunflower is extremely valuable. Its seeds contain the highest level of linoleic acid of any sunflower. Vegetable oils high in linoleic acid are low in saturated fats, which are believed to contribute to heart disease. If serpentine sunflowers were bred with other sunflowers, the saturated fat content might be lower in oil made from the new flowers produced. This could lead to important health benefits.

Puzzle sunflowers are found on only three sites in western Texas and one in New Mexico. This sunflower is unusual because it grows in salty waters. Botanists believe its genes may be useful in creating new types of sunflowers with this characteristic. To preserve the serpentine and puzzle sunflowers' genes, botanists are growing these flowers in greenhouses and storing their seeds.

Schweinitz's sunflowers are found in just a few areas of North and South Carolina. These rare sunflowers posed a baffling mystery for South Carolina botanists who unsuccessfully searched for them throughout the state for more than twelve years. Then in 1986, a group of botanists accidentally came across the rare flowers while ex-

Schweinitz's sunflower

amining soil samples in which some midwestern prairie plants were seen growing.

Recently, Schweinitz's sunflowers grown in greenhouses were replanted on property belonging to a South Carolina power company. A botanist had discovered several types of prairie plants directly along a power line, but although the conditions seemed ideal for its growth, Schweinitz's sunflowers were not among them. With the power company's permission, botanists and volunteers planted eighty-two of these rare flowers at the site.

A plant dug up to show the roots

WESTERN LILY
(Lilium occidentale)

The western lily is among the most beautiful flowers in the Pacific Northwest. The plant stands between 2.5 and 3.5 feet (.65 to .95 m) tall and bears a single nodding blossom. Its deep red flower has a green center and is dotted with maroon specks. But, unfortunately, these showy blossoms have nearly disappeared.

The western lily is now found only in parts of northwestern California and southwestern Oregon. Often these flowers were displaced by housing needs and highway development. Sometimes their natural habitats were turned into farmland. Cattle and deer also overgrazed at many flower sites. Even western lilies growing on government land were sometimes destroyed. In an Oregon state park, a public restroom was mistakenly built on a plot of land where these flowers grew. To make matters worse, because of its beauty, the blossom has frequently been overpicked.

Realizing that the western lily is in serious danger, botanists have banded together to try to both preserve the flower in nature and grow it in greenhouses. So far, they have stored more than 3,000 seeds and are growing

Western lily

Western lily

over 100 western lilies as part of a national collection of endangered plants. When these western lilies bloom in midsummer, the public is invited to view the brilliant blossoms. This lovely small collection gives us a glimpse of what would be lost if these flowers were to become extinct.

DWARF ILIANUS
(Wilkesia hobdyi)

The dwarf ilianus is a branching shrub that stands less than 3 feet (.9 m) tall. It blooms throughout the year. The shrub is found only on the rocky coastal ridges of the Hawaiian island of Kauai. A more abundant relative of the dwarf ilianus is the common ilianus (*Wilkesia gymnoxiphium*), which is branchless and grows to a height of 16 feet (4.87 m). Unlike the dwarf ilianus, its common cousin only flowers once before dying.

The dwarf ilianus was discovered in 1986 during an island-planting project by a forest ranger on his lunch break. The ranger noticed an ilianus that seemed "different" growing on the decaying rock surface of a cliff. It was later learned that the ranger had come across a formerly unknown shrub.

Botanists have since discovered that only about 350 of these rare shrubs exist. Because they grow on the island's high crumbling rock cliffs, they are largely shielded from human harm. But its tall rugged environment did not protect the dwarf ilianus from wild goat grazing. In recent years, the problem worsened due to Hawaii's 1987 law banning goat hunting in order to protect these ani-

Dwarf ilianus

Dwarf ilianus

mals. As expected, the goat population flourished, but at the expense of the dwarf ilianus and other native vegetation. In this instance, efforts to protect one species endangered another.

To preserve the dwarf ilianus, the Pacific Tropical Botanical Garden tried to cultivate the flowering shrub in a greenhouse. Cuttings taken from the cliffside plants were rooted by botanists. But like many native Hawaiian plants, the dwarf ilianus didn't thrive in greenhouse pots. Fortunately, those shrubs planted in outdoor botanical gardens fared better. As the dwarf ilianus outdoor collection grows, cuttings taken from healthy plants will be made available to staff members and volunteers willing to grow the shrub in their home gardens. Through this experiment, botanists may best learn what conditions are necessary for the small shrub's survival.

NECHES RIVER ROSE MALLOW
(Hibiscus dasycalyx)

PETERS MOUNTAIN MALLOW
(Iliamna corei)

Plants in the mallow family have attractive five-petaled flowers in various colors. Although a number of different mallows exist, two types—the Neches River rose mallow and Peters Mountain mallow—may soon be extinct.

The Neches River rose mallow, which bears light beige flowers about 2 inches (5 cm) wide, is found in two Texas locations. Sadly, when botanists visited one of the habitats near a roadside park, they found the plants' environment largely destroyed. Two of the three Neches River rose mallows growing there were buried beneath a 6-foot (1.8-m) pile of debris. The remaining plant was so badly damaged that it took the researchers more than a half hour to find it. Little more than the plant's stalk was left standing and there were no seeds to replant.

The disappointed botanists took cuttings from the remaining plant, hoping to grow new plants. They also scouted the nearby terrain for Neches River rose mallows they might have previously missed. Although several ad-

Neches River rose mallow

Peters Mountain mallow

ditional plants were discovered, their location in a rapidly developing area makes their survival unlikely. Cuttings taken from the newly found plants were rooted along with those from the other Neches River rose mallow. The new plants will be cultivated in greenhouses and botanical gardens under the careful eye of researchers, who will store their seeds away safely. The new seeds will be available for planting if these flowers disappear in the wild.

Peters Mountain mallow is another extremely rare plant. These mallows grow 4 to 5 inches (10 to 12.7 cm) tall and have light pink flowers. They thrive in the thin shallow soil of sandstone bedrock and are found only on Peters Mountain near Narrows, Virginia.

While the Peters Mountain mallow was first identified more than sixty years ago, only three or four of these plants remain alive today. The plant was hurt by a number of factors. Besides not reproducing well in nature, it also was grazed by mountain goats and overpicked by humans.

To protect the last few plants from animals, botanists built wire cages around them. Scientists and volunteers also searched the surrounding leaf litter for additional seeds from which new plants might be grown. Large soil samples were taken, and when the dirt was carefully sifted through a strainer, over 150 seeds were collected.

Researchers are growing these plants in greenhouses, as well as studying them at the Peters Mountain site.

OKEECHOBEE GOURD
(Cucurbita okeechobeensia)

As a relative of the squash and pumpkin, the Okeechobee gourd might seem like any gourd found in a vegetable garden. Yet it is unlikely that you'll come across it, since this plant is nearly extinct.

Years ago the gourd grew abundantly along the shorelines of Lake Okeechobee in the Florida Everglades. But its natural habitat was destroyed when dikes and drainage ditches were constructed for flood control and to *irrigate* nearby farms.

Reshaped by humans, the lake's natural water levels rose, drowning much of the surrounding vegetation. Among the plants that didn't survive were the apple custard tree and others that had supported the Okeechobee gourd's vines. Even worse, now the soil was too waterlogged for new seeds to sprout. While the gourds might have grown again in dry areas along the newly built canals, these regions were routinely sprayed with a *herbicide* to prevent overgrown weeds from clogging the waterways.

To try to save the gourd, botanists took a canoe trip along Lake Okeechobee's shores to search for gourd seeds

Okeechobee gourd

to replant. It was especially important to them to save the gourd because this plant resists *mildew*. It would be useful in breeding programs to try to transfer this quality to foods we eat.

A total of nine seeds were collected on the trip. They were sent to the Bok Tower Gardens, a botanical garden near the gourd's natural habitat. Each of the nine seeds was carefully planted in its own pot. The seeds provided six plants. Eventually, the botanists had eleven healthy gourds. It is hoped that these plants will yield the seeds to keep the Okeechobee gourd alive.

PITCHER PLANT
(Sarracenia purpurea)

The pitcher plant, which may grow up to 3 feet (.9 m) tall, has hollow leaves shaped like a hooded pitcher. The hood and upper part of the leaf are covered with downward-pointing hairs or bristles. The plant produces a reddish purple flower that usually blooms between May and August.

Pitcher plants are unusual because unlike most vegetation, they eat insects and other small animals. These include grasshoppers, crickets, and snails. The plant produces a nectar that attracts its prey. The insects and small animals become trapped in the plant's leaves, or "pitchers." Once the prey enters the leaf, the bristles make escape nearly impossible. The plant's meal slides down the leaf wall and is digested at the bottom by substances produced by the plant. By mid-fall of each year, the pitcher plant's leaves or pitchers may be half-filled with its prey. Then the plant withers and collapses, spilling its contents on the ground.

The organic remains left by the pitcher plant enrich the soil. This natural fertilizer supports different forms of vegetation that otherwise would not grow in the barren soil of the pitcher plant's natural habitat.

Pitcher plant

Experiments have shown the pitcher plant to be keenly adapted to its environment. When grown in fertile greenhouse soil, these plants switch from catching insects and animals to being nourished through soil nutrients. They even tend to grow fewer pitchers. But when planted in poor soil, the plant sprouts more pitchers with which to fertilize its environment.

Many North American pitcher plants may be found in *bogs* in the southeastern United States. However, these plants are now at risk, as their natural environments become increasingly scarce.

Until the late 1800s, bogs covered thousands of acres on the lower Gulf Coastal plain extending from Florida to Mississippi. But over time, these damp regions were often drained to be turned into farmland or grazing pastures. Although cattle do not eat pitcher plants, they trampled over them while feeding on other vegetation. Increased building construction, *pesticide* use, and other factors also took a heavy toll on bogs.

The forces responsible for the past destruction of bogs continue today. If the trend isn't checked, it's likely that much of the pitcher plant's natural environment will be destroyed by the twenty-first century. There is still much to learn about the fascinating pitcher plant and its habitat. But if steps aren't taken to protect pitcher plant bogs, this information is likely to remain undiscovered.

GLOSSARY

bog—a wet, spongy marsh area

botanist—a person trained in the study of plant life

conifer—any of a large group of trees or shrubs that bears its seeds in cones

cultivate—to plant and tend

cutting—a cutoff part of a plant from which a new plant is grown

endangered—close to extinction

extinction—when all of a particular plant or animal species has died

fungus—a plant that lives off of another plant or animal, sometimes causing disease

greenhouse—a building made largely of glass in which plants are grown and protected

habitat—the region in which a plant or animal lives or is found

herbicide—a poison used to kill unwanted plants and weeds

irrigate—to supply land with water through the use of ditches or other means

mildew—a fungus that causes a plant disease
pesticide—a poison used to kill unwanted insects and animals
species—a group of plants or animals that share common
 traits

FOR FURTHER READING

Brown, Anne Ensign. *Monarchs of the Forest: The Story of the Redwoods.* New York: Dodd, Mead, 1984.

Burnie, David. *Plant.* New York: Knopf, 1989.

Coil, Suzanne M. *Poisonous Plants.* New York: Franklin Watts, 1991.

Dowden, Anne Ophelia. *From Flower to Fruit.* New York: Crowell, 1984.

Fischer-Nagel, Heiderose. *Fir Trees.* New York: Carolrhoda Books, 1989.

Lerner, Carol. *Pitcher Plants: The Elegant Insect Traps.* New York: Morrow, 1983.

————. *Plant Families.* New York: Morrow, 1989.

Overbeck, Cynthia. *Cactus.* Chicago: Lerner Publications, 1982.

Patent, Dorothy Hinshaw. *Flowers for Everyone.* New York: Cobblehill, 1990.

Wexler, Jerome. *Flowers, Fruits, Seeds.* Englewood Cliffs, New Jersey: Prentice Hall, 1987.

INDEX

ABOUT THE AUTHOR

Elaine Landau has worked as a journalist, an editor, and a youth services librarian. She has written over thirty-five books for young people, among them *Tropical Rain Forests Around the World* and *Wildflowers Around the World.*

Ms. Landau believes that saving endangered plants is one of our most important challenges.